Forests

A *Where Are We?* Book

by Chris Arvetis
and Carole Palmer

illustrated by James Buckley

Rand McNally for Kids™
Books•Maps•Atlases

Forests can be classified into groups called *ecosystems*. An ecosystem includes all living and nonliving things. Look at the things that are found in a forest ecosystem.

living things
trees
small plants
flowers
insects
animals
birds

non-living things
soil   sunlight
rocks   water

Every forest ecosystem has five layers.
Each layer has a name that tells what it is.
Forest floor:
This is the bottom layer. It is full of
leaves, twigs, and waste material.

Many years ago, over one half of the land on the earth was covered with forests.
Lots of trees have been cut down or destroyed since then.
Now about one third of the land in the world has forests.

Only one third?

Herb layer:
This layer is just above the forest floor.
It has grasses, ferns, and small animals.

Shrub layer:
This is the third layer. This layer
has small plants and shrubs.

We can divide the forests of the world into five basic kinds. Let's look at the forest area we are in. It is called a *temperate evergreen forest.* This forest is found along coasts where the weather is warm and there is plenty of rainfall. Tree giants like the redwoods grow here.

Understory:
The understory is the fourth layer. This layer has many trees and forest animals.

Canopy:
This layer is the treetops. The canopy layer is like a roof over the forest.

Did you know that we are in a temperate evergreen forest?

Of course!

Temperate evergreen forests contain the world's biggest and oldest trees. One California redwood tree measured 367 feet tall. Many redwoods are over 250 feet tall and can be over a thousand years old.

Sequoias, spruce, and pine grow in the mountainous areas of the temperate evergreen forest.
Deer, bear, raccoon, and woodchucks live here.
There are birds and small animals like the wood frog, muskrat, and snapping turtle.

May I have my towel?

This forest ecosystem has many kinds of evergreen trees that have needles that stay green all year long.

pine

spruce

Now let's look at the North Pole where the climate is very cold. This region is called a *tundra*. Mosses and lichens grow here, and only a few shrubs dot the land.
No trees grow in the tundra.

The climate in the tundra is very cold and dry. Part of the soil remains frozen all year long. This frozen soil is called *permafrost*. The permafrost and the strong winds make living difficult.

Caribou, musk oxen, and wolves live here. Lemmings are the smallest animals on the tundra. When spring comes, other animals can be seen. Ducks, geese, and sandpipers come from the south, and ground squirrels awaken from their winter sleep.

snowy owl

arctic hare   lemming

Below the frozen tundra is another type of forest — the *boreal forest*. *Boreal* means "northern," and this large forest area covers the northern parts of the world. Evergreen trees make up this forest. Spruce, pine, and fir trees rise above mosses, lichens, and some herbs.

The northern part of the boreal forest is also called a *coniferous forest*. Conifers are cone-bearing trees that have needles with waxy coverings to survive the colder climate. Conifers are the most abundant type of tree on the earth.

larch   cedar   hemlock

I had no idea that *boreal* means "northern."

Douglas fir

The forest floor in the boreal forest is covered with pine needles. These needles have acid in them. The acids are washed into the soil by the rain. Plants cannot grow in the soil with so much acid. Boreal forests also have many swampy areas called *bogs* where the ground is wet and spongy.

Wintertime is very cold in the boreal forest. Temperatures may be 40 degrees below zero. Many of the birds migrate to warmer climates before winter comes.

Many of the animals of the temperate evergreen forest also live in the boreal forest. Ducks, owls, and woodpeckers can be seen among the trees. Bears, foxes, moose, and wolves live here as well as beavers, porcupines, and mice.

I love the boreal forest.

Other animals like the brown bears find places to hibernate, or sleep, through the winter. The thick fur of bison, elk, lynx, and wolves protect them from the winter cold.

In the temperate deciduous forest, we enjoy all the seasons.

There are more than 2,500 species of deciduous trees. Some of these trees are very old. When a tree is cut down, the number of rings on the cut trunk tell the age of the tree. There is one ring for each year. A tree with ten rings is ten years old.

Another forest system is the *temperate deciduous forest.* This forest area has warm summers and cold winters. The trees are green in the summer, but they lose their leaves in the winter. Maples, oaks, birches, and walnuts grow here, and there is a wealth of wild flowers and shrubs.

Early settlers destroyed many of the deciduous forests by cutting down trees to clear the land for farming. Trees have also been cut and used to build houses and make furniture. Wood pulp is used in making paper. Wood is also needed for making plastic and cellophane.

Now look at the same forest when the trees begin to turn color. This makes a magnificent sight.

Oh, what beautiful colors!

Compare the trees. The first picture shows the tree in the summer. The second picture shows how it looks when the leaves turn color in the fall. The last picture shows the same tree in the winter after all the leaves have fallen.

hickory

white oak

sugar maple

Birds, big animals like deer and bears, and small animals make their homes in these forests. Many of the animals have small bodies to help them move through the thick forest. Look at all the animals.

Otters, beavers, raccoons, and muskrats are found in the temperate deciduous forests. Deer, squirrels, skunks, opossums, chipmunks, bears, and moose roam through the woods. There are also snakes and lots of birds.

1 bluejay	5 chipmunk	9 fox
2 raccoon	6 woodpecker	10 squirrel
3 bear	7 deer	
4 badger	8 owl	

Trees provide foods. Hazelnuts, walnuts, and pecans are gathered from deciduous trees. The sugar maple is tapped for its maple syrup. A hole is bored in the tree, a rod inserted, a pail attached to the rod, and the syrup is gathered. Maple syrup is used for many purposes.

As many as 150 kinds of trees can be found in a tropical rain forest. The upper canopy is thick so that very little sunlight gets down to the forest floor. Lots of rainfall makes it a very humid place.

Now let's look at the most famous kind of forest — the *tropical rain forest*.
This forest area is near the equator where the climate is wet and very warm.
It has the most kinds of trees. There are broadleaf trees such as the mahoganies and the teaks.
Other plants and vines grow everywhere which makes a thick jungle of plants.

Large tropical rain forests are found in the Amazon River Basin of South America and the Congo River Basin of Africa. People sometimes use the word *jungle* to refer to a tropical rain forest. The junglelike trees are woven with vines, and beautiful flowers can always be found.

cymbidium   lady's slipper

Monkeys, bats, insects, and lizards can be found. Pretty birds like the toucan and the parrot live in the tropical rain forest.

Some of the world's largest snakes and spiders are found in the tropical rain forest. Look at the animals that live in the rain forest.

lower levels
tiger
jaguar
armadillo

mandrill

And very humid!

The tropical rain forest can get very, very hot!

middle levels
ocelot
leopard
gibbon

chimpanzee

upper levels
hummingbird
spider monkey
toucan

emerald tree boa
chameleon
bat

sloth

Tropical seasonal forests are farther away from the equator. There is less rain and some areas have a long dry season. The trees are about 100 feet tall, shorter than those in the tropical rain forests.

tropical seasonal forest

tropical rain forest

A forest that is similar to the tropical rain forest is the *tropical seasonal forest.* This forest has a cooler climate with a wet and dry season.
Some of the trees even shed their leaves during the dry season.
Bamboos and palms are found here.

In Indo-Malaysia seasonal forests, the monsoon rains lead to a thick growth of plant life. In similar areas of Africa and South America, the lack of rain causes less tree growth and shorter trees.

baobab

The tropical forest areas provide lumber, fruit, medicines, gums, resins, and oils.

1 brazil nuts
2 cashews
3 coconut
4 bananas
5 papaya
6 bread fruit
7 lumber
8 gum
9 rubber
10 medicine

1

Many interesting animals roam through the tropical seasonal forest.
Jaguars, leopards, tigers, and small birds and animals can be found.

Grassland areas called *savannas* also have trees.
The trees grow far apart or in clumps.
Giraffes, tigers, lions, and zebras can be found in the tropical savannas, while bears, deer, and elk can be found in the temperate savannas.

Fires have destroyed many forests. Most of the fires are started by people. A few fires are started by lightning. People have also destroyed forests by cutting trees down. When a large forest area is destroyed, it is called *deforestation*.

Many forests have been destroyed, but new forests are also being planted or are beginning naturally. A new forest grows in stages as shown in the pictures. Because it takes years for trees to grow, everyone must work to save the forests.